FLORIDA: PERFECT FOR PALM

Palms are ubiquitous in Florida—in parks, yards, homes and offices, botanical gardens, along roadsides and beaches. This abundance reflects Florida's palm-friendly climate: Both of the state's two climate zones—subtropical in the north and tropical in the south—provide a mix of heat, humidity and rain that allows palms to thrive. Of the roughly 2,600 modern palm species, 12 are native to Florida, and countless other species introduced from tropical regions worldwide flourish there as well.

ANCIENT AND DIVERSE PALM CHARACTERISTICS

DNA evidence indicates that palms likely have been part of the earth's floral landscape for about 135 million years. In that time, some basic palm growth habits evolved: Many familiar species are treelike; others resemble shrubs, and a few grow as vines. Palm species that produce a single stem are said to be solitary, in contrast to clustering species in which individual plants have two or more stems. Palm leaves take two forms: broad, fan-shaped, palmate leaves, and slender, feather-shaped pinnate leaves. As flowering plants, all palms produce fruit; examples are the dates and coconuts humans and many other animals enjoy. The fronds of large palms can also be heavy enough to injure bystanders or dent vehicles when they fall, even though palm trunks and fronds are herbaceous.

Beyond these basics, palms are intriguingly diverse. Most species mature at a height of 10–50 ft. (3–15 m), but the tallest may attain a height of 150 ft. (45.7 m) or more. Conversely, dwarf palm species typically top out at 6 feet or less and are often used as house plants. Palms generally thrive in full sun (or bright interior light), but some species require shade, and whereas very cold or freezing temperatures seriously damage or kill most palms, a few hardy species can survive brief periods of snow. There's also considerable variation in palm life histories: Some species grow as much as 4–7 ft. (1.2–2.1 m) per year, whereas others grow extremely slowly and may endure for a century or more, perhaps outliving the humans who planted them.

Measurements denote the height of plants unless otherwise indicated. Illustrations are not to scale.

N.B. – Many edible wild plants have poisonous mimics. Never eat a wild plant or fruit unless you are absolutely sure it is safe to do so. The publisher makes no representation or warranties with respect to the accuracy, completeness, correctness or usefulness of this information and specifically disclaims any implied warranties of fitness for a particular purpose. The advice, strategies and/or techniques contained herein may not be suitable for all individuals. The publisher shall not be responsible for any physical harm (up to and including death), loss of profit or other commercial damage. The publisher assumes no liability brought or instituted by individuals or organizations arising out of or relating in any way to the application and/or use of the information, advice and strategies contained herein.

Waterford Press publishes reference guides that introduce readers to nature observation, outdoor recreation and survival skills. Product information is featured on the website: www.waterfordpress.com.

Text & illustrations © 2022 Waterford Press Inc. All rights reserved. Edited by Timothy K. Broschat, PhD. Photos © Timothy K. Broschat, PhD unless otherwise noted. To order or for information on custom published products please call 800-434-2555 or email orderdesk@waterfordpress.com. For questions or to share comments email editor@waterfordpress.com.

ISBN 978-1-62005-510-6

$7.95 US.

Made in the USA

FLORIDA PALMS

FLORIDA PALMS – A Folding Pocket Guide to Familiar Palms of Florida

Kavanagh/Leung

A Folding Pocket Guide to Familiar Palms of Florida

CLUSTERING

Paurotis Palm
Acoelorrhaphe wrightii
Size: To 30 ft. (9 m)
Type: Clustering
Origin: Southern Florida and Mexico/Central America
Description: Also known as the Everglades palm, it is found in dense stands in swamps of southern Florida. Light green leaves have spiny petioles. Stems are very slender and covered with fibrous matting. The tiny orange fruit turns black when ripe. Grows poorly on limestone soils.

Clustering Fishtail Palm
Caryota mitis
Size: To 25 ft. (7 m)
Type: Clustering
Origin: Southeast Asia
Description: This clustering palm is named for the light green, fishtail-shaped leaflets on its bipinnate leaves. After 10–20 years, the stems will produce large clusters of dark reddish fruits followed by death of the entire palm.

Cataract Palm
Chamaedorea cataractarum
Size: To 6 ft. (2 m)
Type: Clustering
Origin: Southern Mexico
Description: Glossy dark green foliage forms a nice clump. Grows best in shady sites.

European Fan Palm
Chamaerops humilis
Size: To 12 ft. (3.5 m)
Type: Clustering
Origin: Mediterranean coast
Description: Bushy evergreen palm forms a multi-stemmed rounded shrub or single stemmed small tree. Leaves are fine-textured silver-green fan-shaped leaves up to 24 in. (60 cm) across. Petioles are very spiny. Grows best in central and north Florida.

CLUSTERING

Areca Palm
Dypsis lutescens
Size: To 30 ft. (9 m)
Type: Clustering
Origin: Madagascar
Description: This clustering palm grows a dozen or more slender, green, ringed trunks. Stems are topped with about a half dozen downward-curving green leaves with a foot-long crownshaft that varies from green in healthy palms to golden-orange in nitrogen deficient palms. Yellow flowers bloom in summer, followed by small yellow-orange fruits.

Senegal Date Palm
Phoenix reclinata
Size: To 30 ft. (9 m)
Type: Clustering
Origin: Africa
Description: This huge clumping palm produces multiple stems with a canopy spread up to 30 ft. (9 m) across. Individual stems have a knobby appearance. Produces large numbers of orange dates that unfortunately germinate as weeds.

MacArthur Palm
Ptychosperma macarthurii
Size: To 16.5 ft. (5 m)
Type: Clustering
Origin: Australia and New Guinea
Description: This clustering species has very slender stems (2 in. (5 cm) or less) and a small crown of fine-textured leaves. The small, pea-sized red fruits germinate readily.

Needle Palm
Rhapidophyllum hystrix
Size: To 6 ft. (2 m)
Type: Clustering
Origin: Southeastern US
Description: Shrubby nearly trunkless clumping fan palm. Noted for its large palmate green leaves. Named in reference to the long stiff needle-like black spines that project from the leaf bases. Grows best in shady sites in central and north Florida

© Shutterstock

CLUSTERING

Lady Palm
Rhapis excelsa
Size: To 10 ft. (3 m)
Type: Clustering
Origin: Southern China and Taiwan
Description: Spreads by underground rhizomes forming dense multi-stemmed clumps with glossy dark green fan-shaped leaves divided into broad ribbed segments. Leaflet tips are saw-toothed. Grows best in shady sites.

Saw Palmetto
Serenoa repens
Size: To 10 ft. (3 m)
Type: Clustering
Origin: Southeastern US
Description: Fan-palm has leaves that form a rounded fan of about 20 leaflets. Leaf stems have saw-tooth like projections that can cut human flesh. These palms form large shrubby thickets and provide important habitat for wildlife in Florida's palmetto prairies.

SOLITARY

Christmas Palm
Adonidia merrillii
Size: To 26 ft. (8 m)
Type: Solitary
Origin: Philippines
Description: This palm has a slender gray trunk with stiff arching green leaves that can grow 4–5 ft. (1.2–1.5 m) long. The common name refers to the clusters of bright red fruits that appear during fall and winter months.

Alexandra Palm
Archontophoenix alexandrae
Size: To 40 ft. (12 m)
Type: Solitary
Origin: Australia
Description: The trunk shows ridged rings as the plant grows, with a smooth green crown shaft about 2 ft. (6 m) long. Leaflets on the 6 ft. (2 m) long leaves are often oriented in a vertical plane rather than horizontally.

SOLITARY

Bismarck Palm
Bismarckia nobilis
Size: To 40 ft. (12 m)
Type: Solitary
Origin: Madagascar
Description: Thick trunk holds silvery-blue, or rarely, light green, palmate leaves that can grow to 4 ft. (1.2 m) across and creating a spread of up to 16 ft. (4.9 m).

Pindo Palm
Butia capitata
Size: To 20 ft. (6 m)
Type: Solitary
Origin: Brazil
Description: This palm has a thick, stout trunk with feathery blue-green leaves that arch downwards. As it grows and ages, the stem will show gray knobby leaf bases.

Carpentaria Palm
Carpentaria acuminata
Size: To 40 ft. (12 m)
Type: Solitary
Origin: Australia
Description: This medium-sized palm has gracefully arched feather leaves and bright red, cherry-like fruits. It is very fast growing.

Florida Silver Palm
Coccothrinax argentata
Size: To 20 ft. (6 m)
Type: Solitary
Origin: Florida Keys and the Bahamas
Description: Distinguished by a slender, smooth trunk, bluish-green, deeply divided palmate leaves with a silver underside and fibrous matting hanging from the crown.

Coconut Palm
Cocos nucifera
Size: To 80 ft. (24.4 m)
Type: Solitary
Origin: Southeast Asia
Description: Identified by its smooth gray trunk, often gracefully curved, and with a large bulge at its base. The leaf bases and immature fruits can be green, bronze, orange, or yellow in color, depending on variety. At maturity (4–6 years) it produces clusters of sweet-smelling flowers followed by the well known coconuts. Highly susceptible to Lethal Yellowing disease.

Hurricane Palm
Dictyosperma album
Size: To 30 ft. (9 m)
Type: Solitary
Origin: Mascarene Islands
Description: Medium sized palm with 6 in. (8 cm) thick ringed trunk topped with an 8 ft. (2.5 m) wide canopy of stiff medium green leaves. New leaves of some varieties emerge reddish.

Spindle Palm
Hyophorbe verschaffeltii
Size: To 12 ft. (3.5 m)
Type: Solitary
Origin: Mascarene Islands
Description: Smooth gray trunk is fairly thick (1 ft. (30 cm)) for the size of the palm and often bulges in the middle. Rather stiff 3–4 ft. (1–1.2 m) long light green leaves arise from a smooth green crownshaft at the top of the trunk.

Red Latan Palm
Latania lontaroides
Size: To 40 ft. (12 m)
Type: Solitary
Origin: Mascarene Islands
Description: Trunk is clean, relatively slender, and slightly swollen at base. Large, fan-shaped silvery green leaves are reddish in very young palms. Very similar to Bismarck Palm, but smaller and less cold tolerant.

Ribbon Fan Palm
Livistona decora
Size: To 40 ft. (12 m)
Type: Solitary
Origin: Australia
Description: Named for its deeply divided fan-shaped leaves that look like drooping ribbons. The straight gray trunk shows prominent leaf scar rings.

Canary Island Date Palm
Phoenix canariensis
Size: To 40 ft. (12 m)
Type: Solitary
Origin: Canary Islands
Description: This solitary growing flowering plant can spread to 20 ft. (6 m) wide. Whitish flowers are followed by small yellow to orange dates in summer. Highly susceptible to Lethal Bronzing and Fusarium Wilt diseases.

Sylvester Palm
Phoenix sylvestris
Size: To 50 ft. (15 m)
Type: Solitary
Origin: Southern Asia
Description: Also known as the Wild Date Palm it is similar to the edible date palm. Its fat trunk resembles the skin of the pineapple due to the shape of the persistent leaf bases.

Buccaneer Palm
Pseudophoenix sargentii
Size: To 10 ft. (3 m)
Type: Solitary
Origin: Florida Keys and the Caribbean
Description: Identified by its slender, ringed, gray trunk. Fronds are blue-green in color and up to 5 ft. (1.5 m) long. Slow growing.

Dwarf Palmetto
Sabal minor
Size: To 6 ft. (2 m)
Type: Solitary
Origin: Florida
Description: This small species of palm has large fan-shaped leaves and no visible trunk

Cabbage Palm
Sabal palmetto
Size: To 65 ft. (19.8 m)
Type: Solitary
Origin: Southeastern US
Description: The state tree of Florida, it is a highly tolerant tree surviving salt spray, cold, drought, and temporary flooding, but is highly susceptible to Lethal Bronzing disease. It has green fan-shaped leaves and often an attractive lattice-like pattern of persistent leaf bases on the trunk.

Windmill Palm
Trachycarpus fortunei
Size: To 10 ft. (3 m)
Type: Solitary
Origin: China
Description: Small palm with deeply divided, fan-shaped leaves. Trunk may be covered with black hair-like fibers from old leaf sheaths. Grows best in north and central Florida

Montgomery Palm
Veitchia arecina
Size: To 50 ft. (15 m)
Type: Solitary
Origin: Southeast Asia
Description: Tall, fast-growing palms with attractive, rather straight, dark green leaves and bright red fruits at the bottom of the crown.

Triangle Palm
Dypsis decaryi
Size: To 30 ft. (9 m)
Type: Solitary
Origin: Madagascar
Description: A medium-sized palm with a distinctive crown of blue-green, keeled, feather leaves. The leaves grow in 3 planes giving the crown base a triangular shape.

Bottle Palm
Hyophorbe lagenicaulis
Size: To 10 ft. (3 m)
Type: Solitary
Origin: Mauritius
Description: A relatively short palm, it is distinguished by its smooth, grayish-white bottle-shaped trunk. Short (3–4 ft. (1–1.2 m)) fronds sit atop a slender green crownshaft.

Keys Thatch Palm
Leucothrinax morrisii
Size: To 30 ft. (9 m)
Type: Solitary
Origin: Florida Keys and the Caribbean
Description: Fan-shaped palmate leaves grow on a slender, often fiber-covered stem. Leaves are pale yellow-green or blue-green in color and fruits are small and white in color.

Chinese Fan Palm
Livistona chinensis
Size: To 50 ft. (15 m)
Type: Solitary
Origin: Japan, China and Taiwan
Description: Classified as an invasive species in some parts of Florida, tree is deep-green or bluish-green when young. Fan-shaped leaves lose spines over time. Yellow blooms emerge in clusters, followed by blue-green oblong fruits.

Edible Date Palm
Phoenix dactylifera
Size: To 50 ft. (15 m)
Type: Solitary
Origin: North Africa and Middle East
Description: This large palm is the source of edible dates. The heavy trunk is covered in distinctive diamond-shaped leaf bases while the stiff blue-green leaves have long sharp spines at the bases.

Pygmy Date Palm
Phoenix roebelenii
Size: To 20 ft. (6 m)
Type: Solitary
Origin: Southeast Asia
Description: Small single-stemmed palm is often planted in groups giving it the appearance of being multi-trunked. Leaves are feather-shaped with 2–3 in. (5–7 cm) long spines at their bases. Mature palms have knobby and usually crooked trunks.

Solitaire Palm
Ptychosperma elegans
Size: To 20 ft. (6 m)
Type: Solitary
Origin: Australia
Description: Slim light gray or white trunk grows to a maximum diameter of 4 in. (10 cm). This single-stem palm is often planted in clumps giving the appearance of a clustering species.

Royal Palm
Roystonea regia
Size: To 100 ft. (30 m)
Type: Solitary
Origin: Southern Florida and Cuba
Description: This massive palm is best for street plantings and commercial landscapes. Leaves can be up to 12 ft. (3.5 m) long with a smooth green base called the crownshaft. This palm is considered self-cleaning as the dead old leaves drop off naturally. Due to their weight, these falling leaves can be hazardous to people and property.

Queen Palm
Syagrus romanzoffiana
Size: To 50 ft. (15 m)
Type: Solitary
Origin: South America
Description: This fast-growing palm has a single smooth trunk, glossy, dark green leaves with leaflets in multiple planes. Large orange fruits can be messy. Highly susceptible to Fusarium Wilt disease and grows poorly on alkaline soils.

Florida Thatch Palm
Thrinax radiata
Size: To 20 ft. (6 m)
Type: Solitary
Origin: Florida Keys and the Caribbean
Description: This skinny palm tree has a single slender trunk and a crown of up to 10 palmate leaves.

Mexican Fan Palm
Washingtonia robusta
Size: To 100 ft. (30 m)
Type: Solitary
Origin: Mexico
Description: Also known as Washingtonia, this fast-growing palm tree is native to northwestern Mexico. Fan-shaped leaves have spiny petioles. Highly susceptible to Fusarium Wilt disease.

Foxtail Palm
Wodyetia bifurcata
Size: To 30 ft. (9 m)
Type: Solitary
Origin: Australia
Description: Similar to the massive Royal palm, it is identified by its bushy arching fronds growing from the top of a light gray trunk. Large egg-sized and shaped red fruits can be messy.